WHEN DINOSAURS LIVED

Pterodactyls

KATE RIGGS

Published by
CREATIVE EDUCATION

P.O. Box 227, Mankato, Minnesota 56002
Creative Education is an imprint of The Creative Company
www.thecreativecompany.us

Design and production by Danny Nanos of Gilbert & Nanos
Art direction by Rita Marshall
Printed by Corporate Graphics in the United States of America

Photographs by Alamy (Blickwinkel, Chuck Eckert, INTERFOTO),
Bridgeman Art Library (English School), Corbis (Jonathan Blair), Getty Images
(DEA Picture Library, Image Source, Ken Lucas), Library of Congress

Library of Congress Cataloging-in-Publication Data
Riggs, Kate.
Pterodactyls / by Kate Riggs.
p. cm.
Summary: A brief introduction to the flying pterodactyls,
highlighting their size, habitat, food sources, and demise. Also included is a
virtual field trip to a museum with notable pterodactyl fossils.

Includes bibliographical references and index.
ISBN 978-1-60818-117-9

1. Pterodactyls—Juvenile literature. I. Title.

QE862.P7R546 2012

567.918—dc22   2010049331

CPSIA: 030111 PO1451

FIRST EDITION

2 4 6 8 9 7 5 3 1

CREATIVE EDUCATION

Table of Contents

Pterodactyls were flying reptiles. They lived from about 150 to 65 million years ago. The name pterodactyl means "wing finger."

Pterodactyls lived at the same time as the dinosaurs

Pterodactyls had long wings, thin necks, and short tails. One pterodactyl species called *Pterodactylus* had long, powerful jaws with lots of sharp teeth. Pterodactyls could fly, but they were not birds. They did not have feathers like birds do today.

Pterodactyls had hollow bones
like today's birds have

SOUND IT OUT

Pterodactylus: teh-roh-DAK-til-us

Pterodactylus weighed 2 to 10 pounds (0.9–4.5 kg). Other pterodactyls were as big as vultures. They were about 40 inches (102 cm) long and weighed about 20 pounds (9.1 kg). The largest pterodactyls weighed more than 200 pounds (91 kg)! After a pterodactyl hatched, it grew quickly and started flying.

Remains of the biggest pterodactyls were not found until 1971

Many pterodactyls lived near lakes or seas. They flew over forests and flat places called plains. Pterodactyls could move faster and travel farther than dinosaurs could. But sometimes they walked on land. Some scientists think pterodactyls were able to swim, too.

Pterodactyls had good eyesight and could see from far away

Pterodactyls ate mostly fish and other animals from lakes and seas. Some kinds of pterodactyls lived close to each other. *Pterodactylus* and *Cycnorhamphus* (meaning "swan-like beak") were neighbors.

Some pterodactyls had sharp teeth for catching fish

SOUND IT OUT

Cycnorhamphus: *sik-nor-HAM-fus*

Pterodactyls spent their time flying around looking for food. Their big eyes helped them see prey from far away. Pterodactyls died out about 65 million years ago. That was when the dinosaurs died out, too.

A pterodactyl's wings were leathery and thin but tough

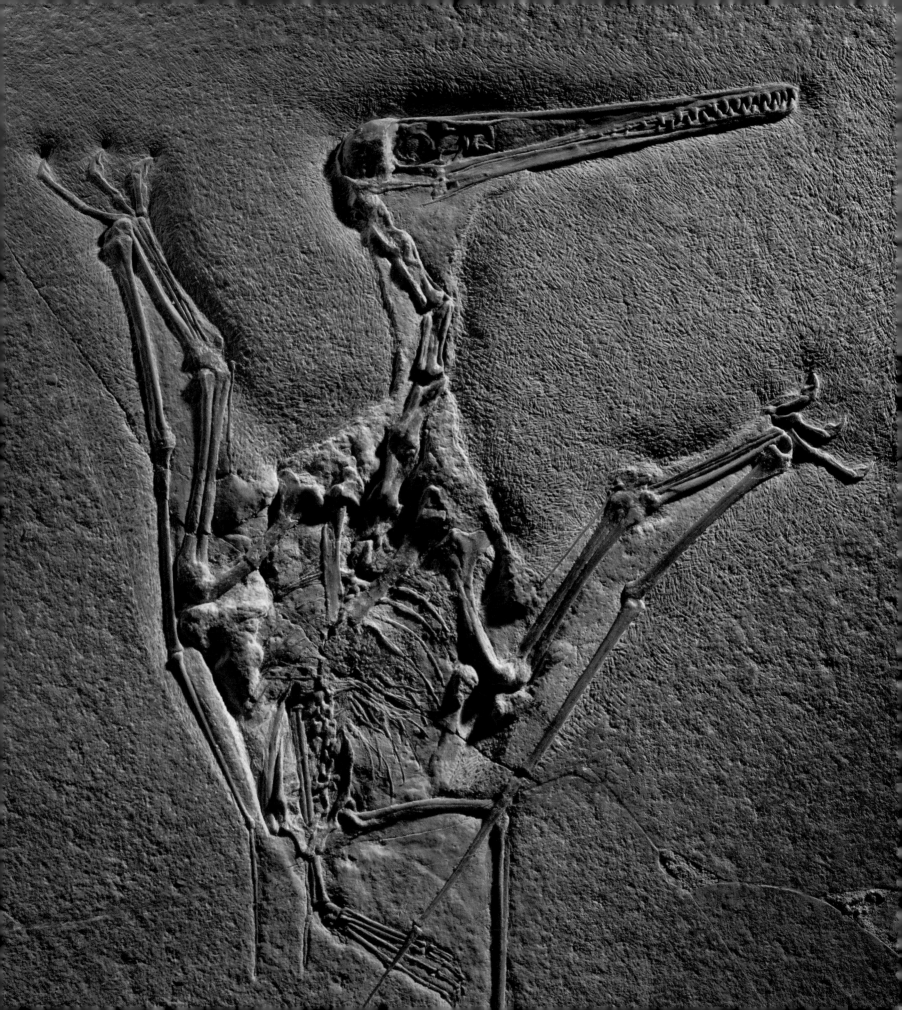

Scientists know about pterodactyls because they have studied fossils. Fossils are the remains of living things that died long ago. Many fossils of *Pterodactylus* have been found in Germany. The first one was found in 1784.

Many fossils are found in a kind of rock called limestone

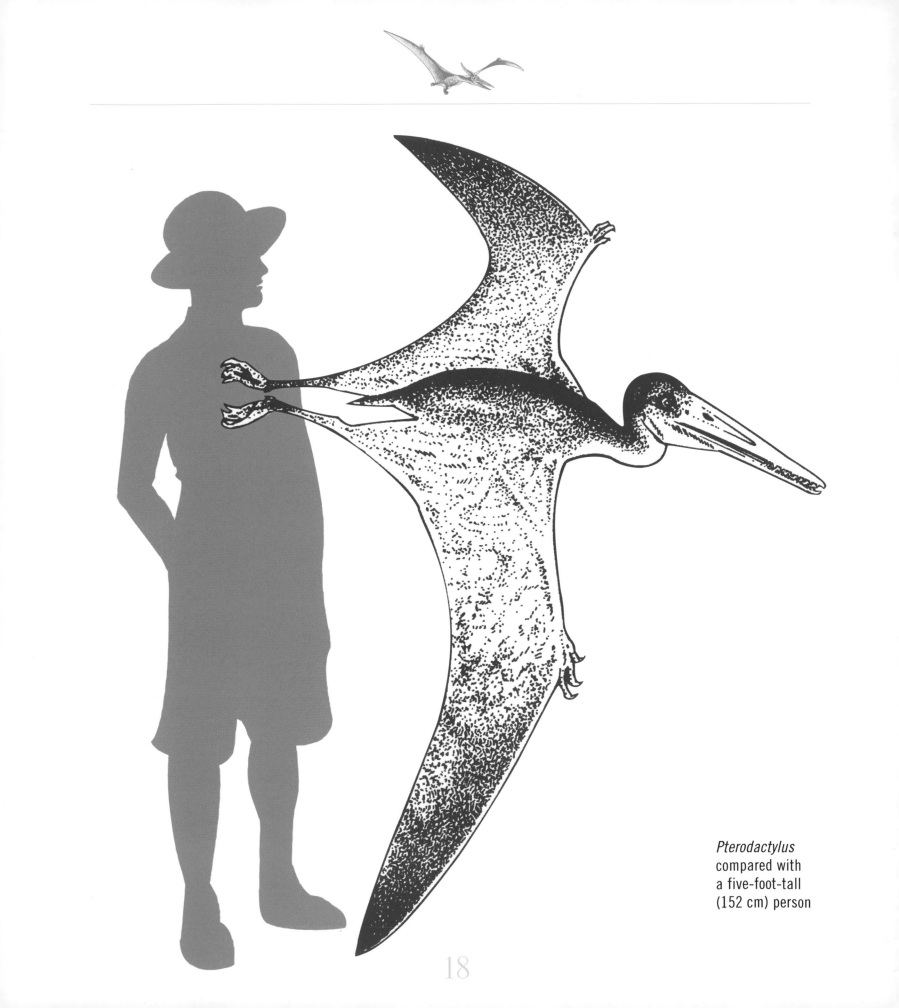

Pterodactylus
compared with
a five-foot-tall
(152 cm) person

French scientist Georges Cuvier thought of the name "pterodactyl." He learned that pterodactyls were related to other reptiles. At first, other people did not believe him. They did not think reptiles could fly.

People used to think that ptero-dactyls could fly only by dropping down from something, like a tree. Now people think they could have flown by lifting off from the ground. But scientists still study pterodactyls. There are more things to learn about this "wing finger"!

This older picture shows a pterodactyl looking like a bat

A Virtual Field Trip: Bürgermeister Müller Museum, Solnhofen, Germany

You can see fossils of pterodactyls at the Bürgermeister Müller Museum in Germany. The museum is in Solnhofen, a town where many fossils have been found. The area used to be covered by water. When some pterodactyls died, they ended up in the water. After a long time, the water dried up into mud, and the mud later became rock. This made the animals into fossils.

Glossary

hatched—came out of an egg

prey—animals that are killed and eaten by other animals

reptiles—animals that have scales and a body that is always as warm or as cold as the air around it

species—a group of living things that are of the same kind

Museums all over the world have models of pterodactyls

Read More

Dixon, Dougal. *Prehistoric Skies*. Mankato, Minn.: NewForest Press, 2011.

Johnson, Jinny. *Pteranodon and Other Flying Reptiles*. North Mankato, Minn.: Smart Apple Media, 2008.

Web Sites

Enchanted Learning: Pterodactylus

http://www.enchantedlearning.com/subjects/dinosaurs/dinos/Pterodactylus.shtml
This site has *Pterodactylus* facts and a picture to color.

PaleontOlogy: Finding Fossils

http://www.amnh.org/ology/index.php?channel=paleontology#features/stufftodo_paleo/findfossils.php?TB_iframe=true&height=500&width=600
This site shows you how to collect your own fossils, like the ones found of pterodactyls.